100

THINGS TO DO IN
HOUSTON
BEFORE YOU
DIE

100

THINGS TO DO IN
HOUSTON
BEFORE YOU
DIE

A.J. MISTRETTA

REEDY PRESS

Library of Congress Control Number: 2015942716

ISBN: 9781681060125

Design by Jill Halpin

Cover Image: Visit Houston

Printed in the United States of America
15 16 17 18 19   5 4 3 2 1

Please note that websites, phone numbers, addresses, and company names are subject to change or cancellation. We did our best to relay the most accurate information available, but due to circumstances beyond our control, please do not hold us liable for misinformation. When exploring new destinations, please do your homework before you go.

CONTENTS

• •

• •

DEDICATION

For my parents, who gave me the crazy idea that I could tackle anything I put my mind to.

And for the people of Houston, who have welcomed this Louisiana boy with open arms and made me one of their own.

● ●

PREFACE

I'll be honest—I didn't think much of Houston growing up. I was a child of New Orleans, the sister city on the Gulf Coast, and my worldview of Houston was of a major metropolis with a big shopping mall (The Galleria) and a bigger amusement park (the now-closed AstroWorld). After launching a career in journalism, I found myself writing for newspapers and magazines in Texas when a former colleague called to offer me a corporate gig in Houston. The money was good, and on my first real visit to the city, I found it charming—not in any traditional way, but rather in its unassuming, make-no-apologies attitude. Here was a city filled with people doing what they do, uninterested in trying to prove anything to anyone. If you like it, here it is, and we'd love to have you. If you don't, no sweat. The door's thataway.

About a year after I arrived in Houston, I truly felt at home. I had found a great group of friends, become active in the community, and started volunteering. Then I got the job of a lifetime doing PR for my new city as part of the visitors' bureau. Five years later, I continue to do this job that I love, representing a unique and thriving place.

Long a business-minded city, Houston has finally come into its own as a destination as well. The word has reached outsiders about the city's long-prosperous arts scene and newer, though no less robust, food scene. Today, Downtown is booming like never before, with new restaurants, bars, and nightlife, attracting thousands of new residents in gleaming high-rises. Neighborhoods from Montrose to the Museum District and Uptown to the East End are experiencing unprecedented development and new investment. And parks are alive with these new people, stretching along the bayous and the greenbelts that wend their way through this urban landscape. It's a great time to be in Houston, whether you're living here or just visiting.

I'm excited to share these 100 things with you. They come from years of experience guiding people on the best events, attractions, spaces, and experiences in H-Town. Cliché though it may be, the beauty of a city as vast and diverse as Houston is that there truly is something for everyone—whether you seek fine art or kitsch, four-star restaurants or dives, the great outdoors or—yes—a seven-mile underground tunnel. So let's go on an adventure together, shall we?

FOOD AND DRINK

SIP AND SAVOR
ON THE TEXAS BLUEBONNET WINE TRAIL

Who needs Napa? You can find great wines along the Texas Bluebonnet Wine Trail, which starts just a half hour northwest of downtown Houston. Take in fantastic views and savor award-winning wines at seven Southeast Texas wineries that dot the map between I-45 and US Highway 290. Whether it's Messina Hof Winery in Bryan or Saddlehorn Winery in Burton, you'll discover Lone Star vintages for every palette, from bold reds to sweet Rieslings. Several of the wineries along the trail offer lodging accommodations, and most do regular special events including seasonal grape stomps, concerts, and wine dinners.

texasbluebonnetwinetrail.com

TIP

Looking for one of the best
views in Texas? Bernardt's
Winery in Plantersville features a
Tuscan-style hilltop tasting room
that overlooks the surrounding hills
and valleys—a perfect place to
sip away the afternoon.

COOK IT UP
WITH MONICA POPE

Award-winning chef Monica Pope has been a star on the local food scene for more than a decade, with concepts such as the Sixth Ward barbecue joint, Beavers, and her globally inspired Sparrow Bar + Cookshop in Midtown. She was once named one of the best new chefs in the country by *Food & Wine* magazine and even competed on *Top Chef Masters*. But although she loves to cook, Pope also enjoys sharing her skills with others through regular cooking classes. In a studio kitchen upstairs at Sparrow, she leads a weekly one-hour class focused on fresh, locally sourced ingredients available at the local farmers' market. And since you'll taste what you prepare, let's just say it's to your advantage to pay attention in class.

3701 Travis St., 713-524-6922
Sparrowhouston.com

Neighborhood: Midtown

DINE ON TOP OF THE WORLD
AT SPINDLETOP RESTAURANT

After suffering serious damage during Hurricane Ike in 2008, Spindletop Restaurant, at the top of the Hyatt Regency downtown, reopened in 2010 to great fanfare. Long a favorite of both residents and visitors, the slow-turning restaurant offers an unobstructed 360-degree view of the city skyline. At thirty-four floors up, patrons can sip a cocktail and enjoy an elaborate meal prepared by one of the Hyatt brand's top culinary teams. The menu changes seasonally, using local ingredients whenever possible. The restaurant's signature dish is its paella with black mussels, fish, shrimp, chorizo, and lobster. *Delicioso*.

1200 Louisiana St., 713-375-4775
hyatt.com/gallery/spindletop

Neighborhood: Downtown

EAT KOREAN-STYLE DUMPLINGS
AT UNDERBELLY

The menu at Chris Shepherd's restaurant, Underbelly, changes daily. And we're not talking a dish added here or subtracted there. Shepherd seeks to tell the story of Houston through the food he serves at the Montrose eatery, from the city's coastal geography to the many different global cultures that call this place home. Inspired by the restaurateurs of small ethnic eateries in Chinatown, Long Point, and beyond, Shepherd turns out creative new dishes based on what's freshest and in season. But the one item that never leaves the menu is the Korean braised goat dumplings. These thick, almost crunchy dumplings mixed with Korean spiced goat, are a must with any meal at this accolade-laden, yet entirely unpretentious, restaurant. They're one of the reasons Shepherd was the first Houston chef to bring home a James Beard Award in more than twenty years.

1100 Westheimer Rd., 713-528-9800
underbellyhouston.com

Neighborhood: Montrose

HAVE A GLASS OF VINO
AT LA CARAFE

Of course it's haunted. What better reason than that to imbibe at the oldest bar in Houston? Entering La Carafe is an exercise in time travel. Hanging on the walls are old portraits, many of people no one knows. The menu is beer and wine only, and cash is the only currency here—don't bother with the plastic. Originally built in 1866, the structure that once housed a bakery and other businesses is timeworn, to be sure. Legend has it that a former bartender named Carl continues to haunt La Carafe, with employees and patrons reportedly hearing the sounds of footsteps and breaking glass from the vacant second story. If the ghost story doesn't get you jazzed, stop by for the cozy ambiance and the jukebox that plays Carole King and Ella Fitzgerald. A vintage cash register reigns over the long bar dripping with candles—the main source of light in the bar.

813 Congress Ave., 713-229-9399

Neighborhood: Downtown

TEST YOUR SKILLS
AT A CHILI COOK-OFF

Think you make a good chili? We'll be the judge of that. Chili cook-offs are a popular pastime in Houston, whether for charity, friendly neighborhood get-togethers, or diehard competitions. Many people will even fight over the question of beans or no beans. Recipes here are passed down from generation to generation, and everyone and their grandma has a secret ingredient. There's a cook-off happening virtually every week. Some are juried while others are open for the public to enter for a fee. Many have a philanthropic angle, with proceeds benefiting a Houston-area nonprofit. Food, competition, good times, and giving back. What's not to love?

CHILI COOK-OFFS

Houston Kosher Chili Cookoff
houstonkosherchilicookoff.com

Firehouse Chili Cook-Off
City of Glenn Heights, Heritage Park

Houston Pod Chili Cookoff
tradersvillage.com/houston/events

Houston Roller Derby Siren Chili Cook-Off
houstonrollerderby.com/index.php/events

YP Chili Cook-Off
www.casahope.org

DIVE INTO OYSTERS
AT GILHOOLEY'S

No pets. No kids. No credit cards. If you're looking for fine dining, keep looking. If you want fresh seafood in a no-frills, come-as-you-are joint, Gilhooley's Oyster Bar is your place. Located in the small seaside community of San Leon, just north of Galveston, Gilhooley's is nothing short of a legendary outpost. In fact, the Travel Channel's Andrew Zimmern named it the "ultimate seafood dive bar." A must try: the Oysters Gilhooley, wood-grilled on the half shell and doused in garlic butter and parmesan cheese. Other favorites include the shrimp gumbo and the seasonal oyster stew (which, according to the menu, is only prepared on days "when it is cold and gray and the cook is in the mood"). With its old license-plate and neon-sign décor, Gilhooley's is certainly a bit off the beaten path, but well worth the journey.

222 9th St., Dickinson, TX, 281-339-3813

Neighborhood: Bay Area Houston

SAVOR THE FLAVOR
AT THE HAUTE WHEELS
FOOD TRUCK FESTIVAL

Food trucks. We love them, but it can be hard to find your favorite. Maybe that's part of the fun—sometimes they're around, and sometimes not. But every spring, dozens of the top trucks in H-Town descend on the Haute Wheels Food Truck Fest. We're talking pizza trucks and cake ball trucks, burger trucks, and even Maine lobster trucks. It's the ultimate mobile food party, and it only happens one weekend a year. Get it while it's hot!

hautewheelshouston.com

EAT BIG
ON LONG POINT ROAD

Houston is a city of international cuisine. And few areas of town showcase that more effectively than Long Point Road. Here you can sample roasted goat at El Hildaguense, Korean barbecue at Korea Gardens, and spicy catfish with basil at Vieng Thai. Dotted with industrial buildings and strip malls, Long Point isn't necessarily a hot spot for tourists, but rather it's a destination for the true foodie interested in trying more authentic, lesser-known restaurants.

Long Point Rd. between Hempstead Highway and Gessner

Neighborhood: Spring Branch

FAST FACT
Houstonians dine out more than four times a week on average, more than residents of any other US city. Maybe that's because there are more than ten thousand restaurants and bars around town, representing more than thirty-five different types of cuisine—from Vietnamese to Indian to Creole.

TOUR TEXAS'S OLDEST CRAFT BREWERY
AT ST. ARNOLD'S

Inside an old warehouse just north of Downtown, you'll find the Lone Star State's oldest craft brewery, St. Arnold's. Visitors climb the stairs of this century-old building to enter a massive German-style beer hall where tastings take place five days a week. For less than ten bucks, you get multiple glasses of seasonal brews and a tour of the production facility to better understand the process used to create some of the label's most popular selections. But while Saint A's is the oldest, it's certainly not alone. These days, Karbach Brewing Co., Buffalo Bayou Brewing Co., 8th Wonder Brewery, and a slew of others are carving out a niche in the local beer landscape. And why not? Texans love their brew as much as they love barbecue brisket and fajitas. In fact, some companies offer motor coach tours to several of the breweries in one afternoon.

2000 Lyons Ave., 713-686-9494
saintarnold.com

Neighborhood: Downtown

GO BRUNCHING
AT HUGO'S

Sunday brunch is a ritual in H-Town. Loud or sophisticated, plated or buffet-style, so long as there's a mimosa or Bloody Mary in hand, it's a certified good time. A favorite among locals is the brunch buffet at Hugo's on Montrose. Mexican-born chef Hugo Ortega offers up an assortment of dishes, from huevos rancheros to frijoles-stuffed empanadas. Finish it all off with churros dipped in hot chocolate.

1600 Westheimer, 713-524-7744
hugosrestaurant.net

Neighborhood: Montrose

OTHER BRUNCH HOT SPOTS

Brennan's of Houston
3300 Smith St., 713-522-9711
brennansofhouston.com

Triniti
2815 S Shepherd, 713-527-9090
trinitirestaurant.com

Neighborhood: Montrose

Royal Oak
1318 Westheimer Rd., 281-974-4752
royaloakhouston.com

Neighborhood: Montrose

Gloria's
2616 Louisiana St., 832-360-1710
gloriascuisine.com

Neighborhood: Midtown

Weights + Measures
2808 Caroline St., 713-654-1970
weights-measures.com

Neighborhood: Midtown

EAT A ZELLAGABETSKY
AT KENNY AND ZIGGY'S

When it comes to larger-than-life personalities, Ziggy Gruber is in a league of his own. The third-generation, New York-bred deli man runs the show at his classic Jewish delicatessen, Kenny & Ziggy's. Walk in to this expansive diner and you're immediately hit by the mixed aroma of cheese blintzes, matzo ball soup, and knishes. Ziggy and a business partner opened the deli in 1999, and it quickly found a following among Houston's robust Jewish community. At their height in the 1930s and '40s, thousands of Jewish delis were spread out across the country, with hundreds in the Big Apple alone. These days, there are far fewer, but Kenny & Ziggy's is a decisive example of the genre, with Ziggy himself often making his rounds among the tables of customers. If you're up for a challenge, order up the Zellagabetsky, a four-pound, eight-decker sandwich on rye, packed with corned beef, pastrami, turkey, roast beef, salami, tongue, and Swiss cheese, then piled up with coleslaw and Russian dressing, and finally topped off with sweet red peppers. Now that's *chutzpah.*

2327 Post Oak Blvd., 713-871-8883
kennyandziggys.com

Neighborhood: Uptown

TASTE THE FLAVOR OF THE CITY
ON A "WHERE THE CHEFS EAT" HOUSTON CULINARY TOUR

It started in 2009 as a way for local chefs to draw attention to the Houston food scene. The idea was for some of the city's most acclaimed culinary masters to show off the places that inspired them. These range from the hole-in-the-wall barbecue and soul food joints to the mom-and-pop Vietnamese and Thai hot spots in Chinatown. Houston Culinary Tours continues going strong, with at least one tour each month led by chefs such as Underbelly's Chris Shepherd, Sparrow Bar + Cookshop's Monica Pope, and the father- and-son team behind Américas restaurants, Michael and David Cordúa. The tours usually take place on a Saturday or Sunday and include transportation and meals at three or more chef favorites. It all happens around themes such as "Barbecue" and "Coastal Seafood" or areas of town such as the Heights or Long Point Road.

Houstonculinarytours.com

CHOW DOWN ON CHICKEN AND WAFFLES
AT THE BREAKFAST KLUB

The line outside the door of the Breakfast Klub on weekends tells you all you need to know about Marcus Davis's Midtown restaurant. Since opening its doors in 2001, the Klub has developed a cult following among lovers of Southern-style breakfast—particularly those seeking a classic version of chicken and waffles. The restaurant itself isn't big, but the waffles are, and that's what counts. The staff could not be more welcoming at this spot, which serves as a de facto meeting spot for the power brokers in Houston's African American community.

3711 Travis St., 713-528-8561
thebreakfastklub.com

Neighborhood: Midtown

TIP

Head to the Breakfast Klub on a weekday morning (the earlier the better) to avoid the crowds you'll find on Saturday and Sunday.

FEAST ON BRISKET
AT KILLEN'S BBQ

Across the country, and particularly in the South, people are passionate about their barbecue. It's the focal point of neighborhood cook-offs, the main dish at family reunions, and the reason for more than a few regional debates over "wet" or "dry." Houstonians take their barbecue seriously, too, and there are plenty of favorites, new and old. One of the best in the area is Killen's Barbecue on Broadway Street in the town of Pearland, south of Houston. People come from miles away to line up for some of Ronnie Killen's brisket, pork ribs, and melt-in-your-mouth baked beans. Ronnie and his team have multiple pits operating around the clock to prepare for the daily onslaught of patrons.

3613 E Broadway, Pearland, TX, 281-485-2272
killensbarbecue.com

OTHER BARBECUE HOT SPOTS

Pizzitola's
1703 Shepherd Dr., 713-227-2283
pizzitolas.com

Neighborhood: The Heights

Jackson Street BBQ
209 Jackson St., 713-224-2400
jacksonstbbqhouston.com

Neighborhood: Downtown

Goode Co. BBQ
5109 Kirby Dr., 713-522-2530
goodecompany.com

Neighborhood: Rice Village

SIP A MARGARITA
ALL OVER TOWN

If Houston had an official cocktail, it would be the margarita. Local Tex-Mex restaurants live and die by their ability to execute one effectively. Too sweet will give you a tummy ache before a buzz. Too sour will have your lips puckering. Too much tequila— well, that comes with its own set of problems. But whether frozen or on the rocks, salt or *sans* salt, when the recipe is just right, it's a beautiful thing. You'll find solid margaritas at bars and restaurants all over town, but a few spots stand out. One is the Original Ninfa's on Navigation, launched by "Mama Ninfa" in 1973 in Houston's East End and still serving a killer marg.

2704 Navigation Blvd., 713-228-1175
ninfas.com

The Pastry War
310 Main St.
thepastrywar.com

Neighborhood: Downtown

Under the Volcano
2349 Bissonnett St., 713-526-5282

Neighborhood: Rice Village

El Tiempo
Multiple locations
eltiempocantina.com

Anvil Bar & Refuge
1424 Westheimer Rd., 713-523-1622
anvilhouston.com

Neighborhood: Montrose

El Big Bad
419 Travis St., 713-229-8181
elbigbad.com

Neighborhood: Downtown

©Visit Houston (photographer: Spenser Harrison)

ARTS AND CULTURE

CATCH A PLAY
AT ALLEY THEATRE

Since its humble beginnings in an old dance theater in 1947, the Alley Theatre has flourished, becoming one of the most respected professional acting companies in the country and debuting more than twenty-five world premieres. The theater's downtown home, opened to the public in 1968, underwent a major renovation in 2015 that elevated its technical capabilities and audience amenities. Each season, the Alley mounts a complete program mixing mostly contemporary American theater with stage classics. Seeing live theater on the 774-seat Hubbard stage or the even more intimate 300-seat Neuhaus stage offers patrons a dramatic experience unrivaled in the region. An annual tradition for many Houstonians is the company's holiday production of Charles Dickens' *A Christmas Carol*.

615 Texas Ave., 713-220-5700
alleytheatre.org

Neighborhood: Downtown

SPEND AN AFTERNOON SIX FEET UNDER
AT THE NATIONAL MUSEUM OF FUNERAL HISTORY

Benjamin Franklin once said that nothing is certain in life but death and taxes. The good news is that at the National Museum of Funeral History, you won't pay taxes on your admission–just on whatever you buy in the gift shop. Though it might sound morbid, this fascinating museum in North Houston painstakingly chronicles the rituals surrounding one of man's oldest cultural customs. Visitors will discover funereal artifacts dating back to ancient times, a fleet of hearses showcasing the vehicle's evolution over the last two centuries, and even a detailed exhibit on the mysterious traditions that surround the death of a pope. One exhibit in the permanent collection explores the funerals of US presidents. It includes the original eternal flame from John F. Kennedy's gravesite in Arlington National Cemetery and a full-scale re-creation of what mourners would have seen at Abraham Lincoln's state funeral.

415 Barren Springs Drive, 281-876-3064
nmfh.org

Neighborhood: Spring

TAKE A TOUR
WITH ARCHITECTURE
CENTER HOUSTON

Houston offers numerous examples of American architecture of the last century, but they're not always easy to find. Enter Architecture Center of Houston. The professionals at ArCH offer weekly walking and cycling tours of some of the city's most interesting neighborhoods, from the cottages and churches of Montrose to the stately Victorian mansions and bungalows of the Heights. Other popular tours include the historic Third Ward, Downtown, the Museum District, and the century-old Rice University campus. These docent-led tours provide specific information about how Houston's architecture was shaped through the decades and what influenced some of the city's most prolific architects. Tours are typically ten dollars per person.

713-520-0155
aiahouston.org

MEET THE FIRST LADY OF TEXAS
AT BAYOU BEND

Perhaps no single person left so indelible a mark on Houston as Ima Hogg. The philanthropist daughter of a former governor, Miss Ima, as she was affectionately known, changed the landscape of the city over the course of the twentieth century. She cofounded the Houston Symphony in 1913, established a major mental health foundation in the 1930s, and worked to remove gender and race discrimination in the Houston school district in the 1940s. One of the biggest gifts she left the people of Houston was her onetime home, Bayou Bend, and its unrivaled collection of American antiques. Nestled on fourteen acres along the banks of Buffalo Bayou in the River Oaks neighborhood (which the Hogg family established) Bayou Bend was designed by famed architect John Staub and completed in 1928. The Bayou Bend collection includes more than forty-seven hundred objects—many collected by Miss Ima herself—showcasing American decorative arts from 1620 to 1870. Surrounding the structure are eight formal gardens that create an urban sanctuary. Miss Ima donated her home to the Museum of Fine Arts, Houston in the 1950s, and it opened to the public in 1966. She passed away in 1975 but not before her legacy of philanthropy earned her the honorary title "The First Lady of Texas."

5201 Memorial Dr., 713-862-5900
bayouonthebend.com

Neighborhood: River Oaks

SEE URBAN ART
AT PROJECT ROW HOUSES

Houston's Third Ward neighborhood became a center for urban art in the early 1990s with the creation of Project Row Houses. Led by co-founder Rick Lowe, a coalition of local artists bought a line of twenty-two shotgun-style houses in the historically poor, mostly African American neighborhood, restored them, and created studios and exhibition space for emerging artists. Today the campus encompasses more than forty restored buildings and includes a residential program for young mothers trying to complete their education. Revolving exhibits are programmed throughout the year, offering new experiences for first-time and return visitors alike. Free docent-led tours of the campus are available on weekends and by appointment during the week.

2521 Holman St., 713-526-7662
projectrowhouses.org

Neighborhood: Third Ward

PAY HOMAGE TO FRUIT
AT THE ORANGE SHOW

"Kitsch" doesn't even begin to describe Jeff McKissack's folk-art monument known as the Orange Show. In 1956, the former postman began work on a project that would honor his favorite fruit. Over the next few decades, he turned a vacant lot in the city's East End into an elaborate architectural masterpiece filled with walkways, mazes, open spaces, mosaics, and exhibits. The Orange Show became a beacon of creativity and artistry in an otherwise depressed neighborhood. After McKissack passed away in the 1980s, a foundation was formed to preserve the Orange Show, which has played host to dozens of concerts, exhibitions, artist talks, and other programs through the years—all aimed at giving the public access to various forms of art. The Orange Show has helped spawn multiple public art projects and one of the most iconic annual events in Houston, the Art Car Parade.

2402 Munger St., 713-926-6368
orangeshow.org

Neighborhood: East End

STUDY AFRICAN AMERICAN MILITARY HISTORY
AT THE BUFFALO SOLDIERS NATIONAL MUSEUM

Beginning with the Revolutionary War, African American soldiers played an active and vital role in the nation's military conflicts. That role is remembered and celebrated at the Buffalo Soldiers National Museum. Founded in 2001 by Vietnam veteran Captain Paul Matthews, the museum contains hundreds of artifacts including uniforms, weaponry, letters, and other items chronicling the experience of black soldiers. In the eighteen hundreds, Native Americans coined the term "Buffalo Soldiers" for black soldiers because they believed the hair of these men resembled the dense matted hair of the buffalo. The museum offers many compelling exhibits, but crowd favorites are the uniforms and other personal objects of African American astronauts.

3816 Caroline St., 713-942-8920
buffalosoldiermuseum.com

Neighborhood: Museum District

ENTER A VEHICLE
IN THE ART CAR PARADE

They come every spring, from as far away as California and Canada. Art cars and their creators descend on Houston each year for the Houston Art Car Parade. Said to be the largest of its kind in the world, the parade features more than 250 cars, with an estimated 250,000 attendees lining the route down Allen Parkway. The Art Car Parade is the epitome of kitschy-cool, drawing a wacky array of folk art on wheels, from unicycles to lawnmowers, and cars to go-carts. Then there's the car that started it all: the 1967 Ford station wagon covered in plastic fruit, now known as the Fruitmobile. These days, the festivities have expanded to include an entire weekend of events, including the irreverent Art Car Ball. Want to enter your vehicle? No sweat—just make sure it's wild enough. With the largest number of resident art cars, Houston is considered the "Art Car Capital of the World." The parade? Well, that just seals the deal.

thehoustonartcarparade.com

Neighborhood: Montrose

SEE A PERFORMANCE
AT MILLER OUTDOOR THEATRE

Miller Outdoor Theatre is one of Houston's brightest cultural gems, offering eight months of free performing arts programming each year. From ballet to symphony, musicals to drama, Miller brings the arts to the masses in a way few other places around the country can. Celebrating more than ninety years of performances, Miller Outdoor is set on a sloping lawn that allows patrons to come and enjoy a performance with their own blanket and picnic in front of a sixty-four-foot stage. Nearly 400,000 people attend performances each year at the theater.

6000 Hermann Park Dr., 832-487-7102
milleroutdoortheatre.com

Neighborhood: Museum District

FAST FACT
Houston is one of only a handful of US cities with resident professional companies in the four disciplines of the performing arts: classical music, ballet, opera, and theater.

SEE FRAGMENTS OF ANCIENT PAPYRUS WRITINGS
AT THE MUSEUM OF PRINTING HISTORY

Ever since early man started drawing on cave walls, we've been communicating with one another via writing. The media, styles, and languages may change with time and place, but our ability to put down words that can then be read by others is one of our greatest gifts. And that's why the Museum of Printing History is so special. Through its permanent and temporary exhibits, the museum tells the story of written communication and how it has affected our lives through the millennia. Starting with Mesopotamian clay tablets and moving through the invention of movable type and on to the printing press, the Museum of Printing History features artifacts important to the evolution of writing and printing. In the Hearst Newspaper Gallery, visitors will find original newspapers chronicling the major events of recent history. Some of the other artifacts you will find include antique bookbinding equipment, Asian movable type, examples of early Asian printing, and fragments of ancient papyrus writings from around the Mediterranean. The museum regularly offers classes in papermaking and bookbinding, as well as lectures and other special events.

1324 W Clay St., 713-522-4652
printingmuseum.org

Neighborhood: Montrose

GO TOE-TO-TOE WITH A BURLESQUE DANCER
AT PROHIBITION

Get ready to step back in time to the Jazz Age. In 2014, the partners behind a local burlesque and cocktail bar concept in the Uptown area decided to move their operation to a historic space in Downtown. That fall, Prohibition opened in the former Isis Theatre space, one of Houston's original silent movie houses, dating back to the early 1900s. Situated just off Main Street, the front area of the space offers an elegant restaurant and bar serving craft cocktails with bite. The food menu is focused around Gulf Coast seafood, with dishes such as char-grilled oysters and flounder *meunière*. To the rear is the beautifully restored theater space where the resident Moonlight Dolls perform. There are classic burlesque and acrobatic shows every weekend in addition to numerous special events throughout the year.

1008 Prairie, 281-940-4636
prohibitionhouston.com

Neighborhood: Downtown

HAVE A MOD TIME
AT RIENZI

Rienzi, the work of noted architect John Staub, was completed in 1954. This stunning space served as the family home of arts patrons Carroll Sterling and Harris Masterson. Set on four lush acres in the tony River Oaks neighborhood, Rienzi is now the center for European decorative arts for the Museum of Fine Arts, Houston. Its collection includes one of the finest assemblages of Worcester porcelain in the United States, along with antique English furniture and European portraits and sculpture. The gardens surrounding the home are yet another attraction, mixing European-style formal gardens with native plants, enhanced by fountains and an Italianate pool. Docent-led tours of the home are offered five days a week, and there is seasonal programming such as classical music concerts and lectures.

1406 Kirby Dr., 713-639-7800
mfah.org/visit/Rienzi

Neighborhood: River Oaks

TAKE IN A LIGHT SHOW
AT TWILIGHT EPIPHANY SKYSPACE

Internationally renowned artist James Turrell has created fascinating installations all over the world using the relationship between natural and artificial light. In 2012, his Twilight Epiphany Skyspace opened on the campus of Rice University, quickly becoming one of the artistic gems of the city. The pyramid-like structure comprised of grass, stone, and concrete uses LED lights in sequence with the rising and setting of the sun to create a dazzling display projected on the structure's ceiling and through a square aperture in the center. The Skyspace draws dozens of people each day to witness how the light slowly changes between sunrise and sunset, altering the patterns within and around the structure. The university's Shepherd School of Music also uses the space as a laboratory for students on certain evenings, making the experience even more extraordinary. Reservations are required to visit the Skyspace, particularly at sunset.

Rice University Campus, 6100 Main St., 713-348-4758
skyspace.rice.edu

Neighborhood: Museum District

DO THE SONG AND DANCE
AT THEATRE UNDER THE STARS

Singing. Dancing. Acting. Most performers would be happy to be great at one of the above, but those who take the stage in Broadway-style musicals are the real triple threat. Theatre Under the Stars began nearly fifty years ago with a single performance. Over the decades, the company has evolved into a full-blown regional music theater company, one of only a handful in the country. Today TUTS offers acclaimed shows straight from New York and world premieres of original works. TUTS performs at least six main stage shows a year at the Hobby Center in the Downtown Theater District, wowing audiences with hits like *The Best Little Whorehouse in Texas*, *Evita*, and *The Music Man*. In 2013, the company launched its TUTS Underground series, which features more contemporary and often avant-garde shows.

800 Bagby St., 713-558-2600
tuts.com

Neighborhood: Downtown

PAY TRIBUTE TO A FOUNDING FATHER OF AVIATION
AT GLENWOOD CEMETERY

With its rolling hills and striking views of the downtown skyline, Glenwood Cemetery is one of the most picturesque spots in the Bayou City. Established in 1871, the massive, eighty-four-acre cemetery serves as the final resting place of many early Houstonians and more recent residents. Ornate mausoleums and garden-like family plots offer serenity—the kind legendary aviation mogul-turned-recluse Howard Hughes sought for his version of forever. The billionaire who built an aeronautical empire and died on a flight from Mexico back to Houston in 1976 is buried beside his parents in a beautiful, yet simple, family plot.

2525 Washington Ave., 713-864-7886
glenwoodcemetery.org

Neighborhood: Sixth Ward

TIP

The cemetery is open daily and can be explored by car or on foot, but to get a real sense of the history of the place and the people interred here, sign up for one of the semi-regular walking tours led by the group Preservation Houston.

COCKTAIL AMONG THE COLLECTIONS
AT THE MUSEUM OF FINE ARTS, HOUSTON

What better way to experience one of the nation's most acclaimed fine arts museums than with your buddies at happy hour? Each Thursday, the Museum of Fine Arts, Houston offers free admission. Package that with a cash-bar happy hour from 6-8 p.m., and you've got the perfect date night or meet-up with friends. The happy hours typically feature a local DJ and bites from a food truck parked just outside the building. With two primary gallery buildings in the Museum District, MFAH is home to more than sixty-five thousand works of art from around the world. The collections span the breadth of recorded time, from antiquity to the modern era, and include some of the most well-regarded groupings of art from Asia and the Americas. You will definitely want to take a stroll through the neighboring sculpture garden as well.

1001 Bissonnet St., 713-639-7300
mfah.org

Neighborhood: Museum District

SEEK INSPIRATION
AT THE CHAPEL OF ST. BASIL

Near the eastern edge of the University of St. Thomas campus, overlooking Montrose Boulevard, is the Chapel of St. Basil. Designed by acclaimed architect Philip Johnson in 1997, the chapel is widely regarded as one of the most architecturally significant buildings in Houston. The structure consists of three essential geometric shapes: a spherical dome, a cube for the body of the church below it, and a granite plane that intersects and connects them. Guests enter the church through a large "tent flap" opening, representing the Tent of Meeting in the Old Testament. Johnson made heavy use of natural light in his design—from the dome to the skylights—intending the progression of light to play off the bare walls of the chapel, constantly changing the interior space. Visitors come to St. Basil to marvel at the space itself, to attend a service, or simply to reflect. In 2006, a prayer garden centered around an intricate labyrinth was added outside the west wall of the chapel, providing yet another space for tranquil reflection.

West Alabama at Montrose Blvd.

Neighborhood: Montrose

FIND YOUR ZEN
AT ROTHKO CHAPEL

When they commissioned the Rothko Chapel, famed French expat arts patrons John and Dominique de Menil wanted a place where Houstonians of all faiths and beliefs could come for a meditative and spiritual experience. Dedicated in 1971, the chapel's distinct, minimalist architecture and interior were inspired by the mural canvasses of Russian-born American painter Mark Rothko. A set of fourteen of these paintings adorns the walls of the intimate chapel, which stands on the edge of the picturesque Menil Collection campus. Each year, more than eighty thousand people from around the world come to pray, reflect, hear lectures, and listen to music. Outside the chapel walls, Barnett Newman's sculpture *Broken Obelisk* is reflected in a shallow pool. The sculpture, dedicated to Dr. Martin Luther King, has stood as a symbol of tolerance and understanding in the Bayou City for more than forty years.

1409 Sul Ross St., 713-524-9839
rothkochapel.org

Neighborhood: Montrose

HIT THE HIGHLIGHTS
WITH A HOUSTON CITYPASS

What are the must-see attractions in Houston? I'm glad you asked. The CityPASS program has pulled together what they believe are the city's top attractions and they're giving them to you for nearly half-off. Houston CityPASS gets you into five attractions: Space Center Houston; the Houston Museum of Natural Science; the Downtown Aquarium; your choice of the Museum of Fine Arts, Houston or Houston Zoo; and a choice of Kemah Boardwalk or Children's Museum of Houston. It's a great way to see some of the best spots in town at a great rate. Each ticket booklet includes one-time admission tickets, detailed attraction info, coupons, and even a map to help you navigate.

Citypass.com/Houston

TIP
Be warned—you have to use
all of the passes within nine days
of starting your adventure.

UNCOVER THE ULTIMATE IN CAMP
AT THE BEER CAN HOUSE

Houstonian John Milkovisch took his love of beer very seriously. So much so that throughout the late 1960s the retired upholsterer turned his small home in the Rice Military neighborhood into an homage to brew, covering the entire house in flattened beer cans, bottles, and other such paraphernalia. Today, the house is one of the city's most recognizable pieces of folk art and perhaps one of the greatest examples of recycling. When you visit, you hear the garlands of beer cans sing in the breeze and imagine Mr. Milkovisch enjoying the pastime that made him a folk-art legend. It's estimated that roughly fifty thousand cans cover the house, most of the contents of which Milkovisch and his family and friends consumed. But the artist was far from picky. When someone once asked him what his favorite label was, Milkovisch replied simply, "whatever's on special."

222 Malone St., 713-926-6368
beercanhouse.org

Neighborhood: Washington Corridor

ABSORB ART
ON GALLERY ROW

For decades, the collection of art galleries on Colquitt Street in the Upper Kirby District have brought some of the most exciting new art and artists to Houston. Known as Gallery Row, this group of more than a dozen galleries spans from the four-decades-old, Texas-focused Moody Gallery to the newer, more avant-garde Nicole Longnecker Gallery. For art buffs, this is the place to be for Saturday evening art openings.

Colquitt St., West of Kirby

Neighborhood: Upper Kirby District

FIND INNER PEACE
AT THE BAPS SHRI SWAMINARAYAN MANDIR

The first traditional Hindu *mandir* of its kind in North America opened just west of Houston in 2004. The mandir is a place of prayer for the followers of Hinduism, but it's also a place of immense beauty and reflection for others. Constructed in sixteen months using 1.3 million volunteer hours, the mandir was created according to ancient Hindu architectural traditions. The white structure is comprised entirely of Turkish limestone and Italian marble. Altogether, there are five towering pinnacles, twelve domes, and 136 marble pillars. More than thirty-three thousand individual pieces were hand carved in India before being shipped to Stafford and put together. Visitors are welcome to tour the mandir daily.

1150 Brand Lane, Stafford, TX, 281-765-2277

FAST FACTS

There are more than three hundred miles of interconnected bike paths and trails spread out across the city of Houston, with many of these running along the city's network of bayous.

HISTORY

STEP BACK IN TIME
AT BATTLESHIP TEXAS

Moored on the Houston Ship Channel beneath the gaze of the San Jacinto Monument is the last dreadnought ship still afloat in the world, the *USS Texas*. Completed more than a century ago, in 1914, the *Texas* saw active combat in both world wars and was a pioneer in advancing radar and gunnery. After playing a critical role in the D-Day invasion and key battles in the Pacific during World War II, the *Texas* became the first battleship memorial museum in the United States in 1948. Visitors can climb onto the guns on her deck, ascend to the various perches around her bridge, and climb below deck to see how thousands of sailors ate, slept, and lived aboard this military vessel. Veterans from around the country, some of whom served on board the *Texas*, come to pay their respects to the ship each year.

3527 Independence Pkwy. South, LaPorte, TX, 281-479-2431
tpwd.texas.gov/state-parks/battleship-texas

Neighborhood: Bay Area

TIP

For the truly adventurous, the *Texas* offers monthly hard-hat tours of areas of the ship unrestored and rarely seen by the public. Warning: lots of climbing and tight spaces involved.

SCAN THE ARCHIVES
AT THE JULIA IDESON LIBRARY

Just across the street from Houston City Hall stands a striking Spanish Renaissance-style building housing some of the most important documents of Houston's past. Originally opened in 1926 as the city's main library, the Julia Ideson building underwent a $33 million renovation in 2010 and reopened its doors to the public. Offering access to rare books, maps, and photographs of Houston and housing the Houston Metropolitan Research Center, the library is dedicated to preserving documents chronicling the city's history. The ornate Texas Room is the library's primary reading room for viewing the HMRC collection. Visitors will find a treasure trove of more than fourteen thousand books on Texas and regional history in addition to maps of Houston and newspapers dating back to the nineteenth century. The Julia Ideson is an architecture-and-history-lover's dream come true. Self-guided tours are available during regular hours, and guided tours are available by appointment.

550 McKinney St., 832-393-1662
houstonlibrary.org/location/julia-ideson-building

Neighborhood: Downtown

BE INSPIRED BY A VESSEL OF SALVATION
AT HOLOCAUST MUSEUM HOUSTON

Holocaust Museum Houston stands as a tool for education and remembrance. The museum chronicles the systematic oppression of Jews and other minority groups perpetrated by the Nazi regime in World War II, from the Nuremberg Laws to the Final Solution. Survivors of the Holocaust who eventually resettled in Houston tell their personal stories through photos, artifacts, and video testimonials in the museum's main exhibit, entitled *Bearing Witness*. One of the more poignant exhibits is an unassuming one: a thirty-seven-foot Danish fishing boat. The vessel is like those used in 1943 by Christians in occupied Denmark to ferry hundreds of Jews to safety in Sweden. One of the few of its kind that remains, it was purchased and brought to the museum in 2008, after a years-long search. The simple craft stands as a physical reminder of the heroism of ordinary people who risked their own lives to save others from certain death.

5401 Caroline St., 713-942-8000
hmh.org

Neighborhood: Museum District

TRACE THE EVOLUTION OF TEXAS RANCH LIFE
AT GEORGE RANCH HISTORICAL PARK

In 1824, more than a decade before the founding of Houston, Henry and Nancy Jones settled on a stretch of land in what is today Fort Bend County. They began a family cattle ranch that was passed down through four generations and grew to more than twenty-three thousand acres. Visitors to the George Ranch Historical Park can trace the history of this land from a time when Texas was still part of Mexico, through the cattle drives of the late eighteen hundreds, and on to the 1930s and '40s, when cattle ranching began to decline. You'll see the historic homes of the family through the decades and perhaps taste authentic food as it would have been prepared in the pioneer days. At the Working Ranch, you can also see cowboys in action, working with their horses to sort and rope cattle as they did a century ago.

10215 FM 762, Richmond, TX, 281-343-0218
georgeranch.org

Neighborhood: Fort Bend County

LEARN HOW TEXAS BECAME TEXAS
AT SAN JACINTO MONUMENT

Rising nearly 570 feet above the Houston Ship Channel, the San Jacinto Monument is the tallest war memorial in the nation. The obelisk, topped by a 220-ton Lone Star of Texas, pays tribute to those who fought on this field and won Texas's independence from Mexico in 1836. The monument and the museum in its base feature many artifacts from the Texas Revolution, from uniforms worn by Mexican commanders to artillery used in key battles. Inside the Jesse H. Jones Theatre, adjacent to the museum, the film *Texas Forever!* offers an overview of the war and the timeline of the Battle of San Jacinto. Visitors can also take an elevator to the top of the monument for a panoramic view of the battlefield, the bustling ship channel, and the city skyline in the distance. Several floors below, the Albert and Ethel Herzstein Library houses a rare collection of books and documents spanning several hundred years and is open to the public and researchers.

One Monument Circle, LaPorte, TX, 281-479-2421
sanjacinto-museum.org

Neighborhood: Bay Area

GET A DOSE
OF THE PAST
AT THE HERITAGE SOCIETY

On the west side of Downtown, under the shadows of City Hall and office skyscrapers, there's a tranquil park that served as the city's first green space. Sam Houston Park offers a respite from the bustle of Downtown, but it also houses some of the most historically significant buildings in the city. The park has served as the home to the Heritage Society since 1954, and over the years that group has relocated architecturally significant homes, a church, and other buildings to the campus to showcase the history of the region. The society also manages a museum that traces Houston's progress from its founding in 1836, to the growing port and railroad city of the nineteen hundreds, through the discovery of oil at Spindletop and the onset of the energy boom. Admission to the museum is free and docent-led, paid tours of the homes are also available.

1100 Bagby St., 713-655-1912
heritagesociety.org

Neighborhood: Downtown

EXPLORE NASA
ON A LEVEL 9 TOUR

In one of the defining speeches of his presidency—delivered at Rice University—John F. Kennedy set forth the bold goal in 1962 that the United States would go to the moon in that decade. Though Kennedy's term in office ended with his tragic death the year after that speech, his vision continued on, and the establishment of the Johnson Space Center and Mission Control in Houston helped NASA put a man on the moon in 1969. Over the decades, Johnson Space Center has served as one of the primary centers of aerospace innovation, from the creation of the Space Shuttle to the next phase of space exploration now being developed. To see the real NASA, take a Level 9 Tour offered by Space Center Houston, the visitor arm of Johnson. Level 9 Tours offer behind-the-scenes access to areas typically off limits to the regular public. The tour takes guests to the historic Mission Control and also to the modern-day control center that helps operate the International Space Station. Other buildings on the massive Johnson campus are also featured on the tour, but availability changes, depending on activities underway.

1601 NASA Pkwy., 281-244-2100
spacecenter.org

Neighborhood: Bay Area Houston

TIP

Level 9 Tours are only available for up to twelve guests each weekday, and all participants must be at least fourteen years of age. Your Level 9 Tour ticket includes admission to the rest of Space Center Houston, from the interactive Astronaut Gallery to the *Independence*, a full-size, explorable replica of the Space Shuttle.

RAIL ABOUT HISTORY
AT MINUTE MAID PARK

A 1913 book by writer Jerome Farber is famous for its title, *Houston: Where Seventeen Railroads Meet the Sea.* The phrase stuck, perfectly describing the nexus of agriculture, manufacturing, and trade the city had become. Today, Minute Maid Park, on the eastern edge of Downtown, continues to reflect Houston's historic relationship with the railroads. Built to incorporate the former Union Station rail hub, the home of Major League Baseball's Houston Astros features a full-size vintage locomotive that runs along a short length of track on the left field wall. The building marries the classic features of the former station with the conveniences of a modern ball field. It even has a retractable roof, allowing fans to enjoy a climate-controlled game on the warmer days of the season. On a tour of the park, offered 10 a.m. to noon Monday through Saturday, guests can explore behind-the-scenes areas like the broadcasting booth, the press box, and the dugout.

501 Crawford St., 713-259-8000
astros.mlb.com/hou/ballpark

Neighborhood: Downtown

FAST FACTS

- "Houston" was the first word spoken from the moon. The 1969 Apollo 11 mission gave the city a permanent place in the history books when astronaut Neil Armstrong spoke the line, "Houston, Tranquility Base here. The Eagle has landed."

- The city of Houston is big. How big? Well, at 655 square miles, Houston could contain the cities of New York, Washington, Boston, San Francisco, Seattle, Minneapolis, and Miami.

©Visit Houston

SPORTS AND RECREATION

TAILGATE WITH THE BULLS
AT A TEXANS GAME

It's little exaggeration to say football is a religion in the Lone Star State. From Friday night lights on the local high school field to a stadium of seventy-five thousand raucous fans on Sunday, weekend worship on the gridiron is a way of life. But then no one does it quite like the fans of the NFL Houston Texans. At every home game, they begin to assemble before dawn around NRG Stadium: encampments of beer-toting revelers cooking up every type of food imaginable. We're not talking hot dogs and burgers, but gourmet feasts of everything from Korean-style BBQ to savory chili. Regardless of how the team performs, these fans are committed to putting on a show fueled by food, drink, and music, and that includes welcoming the fans of the opposing team into the festivities. Perhaps that's why Houston regularly ranks as one of the top NFL cities when it comes to tailgating.

One NRG Park, 832-667-2002
houstontexans.com

Neighborhood: NRG Park

GET CLOSER TO NATURE
AT ARMAND BAYOU NATURE CENTER

Set on roughly twenty-five hundred acres in Houston's Bay Area, Armand Bayou Nature Center is one of the largest urban wilderness preserves in the country. The center covers several different types of natural habitats including prairie, marsh, bayou wetlands, and forest, all home to more than 350 different species of birds and animals. Take a hike on five miles of trails across the preserve or paddle down the bayou itself on a guided tour to see alligators, hawks, deer, and other residents of this diverse ecosystem. For an up-close-and-personal encounter, head to the visitors center, where you'll find displays of live snakes, alligators, and even bison. Nearby, the restored Martyn Farm offers visitors a glimpse of rural farm life in the late eighteen hundreds. Other programming is offered monthly, including guided photo hikes, wildflower tours, and full-moon owl prowls.

8500 Bay Area Blvd, Pasadena, TX, 281-474-2551
abnc.org

Neighborhood: Bay Area

STROLL THE GROUNDS
AT THE JAPANESE GARDEN

In 1992, a new garden was created inside Hermann Park to symbolize the friendship between Japan and the United States and to honor the Japanese community that resides in Houston. Designed by renowned landscape architect Ken Najima, the five-acre Japanese Garden is built in the traditional Daimyo style and offers a tranquil place of reflection and escape, with winding stone paths, bonsai-cut trees, and a pond filled with large koi. Visitors enter through a gate facing the park's reflecting pool and are immediately immersed in the garden's other-worldly aesthetic. Icons abound, including a stone lantern that greets visitors near the entrance to symbolically "light their way" through the garden. At the center of this "stroll garden" is a tea house surrounded by Japanese maples and crepe myrtles.

6001 Fannin St., 713-524-5876
hermannpark.org

Neighborhood: Museum District

TIP
Visit the garden in the spring when its hundreds of azalea trees are in bloom, creating a blanket of bright purple, pink, and white color throughout the grounds.

GET SANDY
AT SYLVAN BEACH PARK

The fine white sand of Sylvan Beach has been drawing visitors to the community of LaPorte on Galveston Bay for more than a century. The closest beach to Houston, the thirty-two-acre Sylvan Beach Park is a recreational hub offering great picnic spots, a children's playground, a fishing pier, a boat ramp, and a skate park. When it comes to ocean breezes, it just doesn't get any better than this.

400 Bay Shore Dr., LaPorte, TX

Neighborhood: Bay Area Houston

PLAY WITH GIANTS
AT FONDE REC CENTER

Basketball court ballers in H-Town know that Fonde Rec Center is the place to go to hone their skills. Pickup games here are legendary, with a number of Rockets players and other former pro players often joining in the action. The Center, just west of Downtown, is a mecca for both kids and adults across the city who want to play with the big boys. But if you want to run the court here, make sure you bring the skills—this isn't your neighborhood pickup game.

110 Sabine St., 713-226-4466
houstontx.gov

Neighborhood: Downtown

STOMP A DIVOT
AT THE HOUSTON POLO CLUB

"The Sport of Kings" is played each spring and fall season at the twenty-six-acre Houston Polo Club. Just a few minutes from Uptown, the club holds matches weekly, with Sunday afternoon finals matches open to the public. If you're not familiar with the rules of polo, no worries. The club's website explains how the game is played and even offers a glossary of terms. Our favorite term? The divot stomp. Between the third and fourth of the six periods of play called "chukkers," there's the tradition of inviting the crowd onto the field to help fix the divots created by the horses' hooves. Then it's back to watching one of the most graceful of games. The club also offers polo classes if you're looking to take up a new sport!

8552 Memorial Dr., 714-681-8571
thehoustonpoloclub.com

Neighborhood: Uptown

LEARN MOVES
AT THE MET

Whether you're an accomplished dancer or an aspiring one with few skills, MET Dance Center in Midtown has a class for you. The MET Dance Company is a Houston-based professional dance troupe that performs multiple times each year in the city and elsewhere around the country. The center is the dance company's sister organization, offering classes in everything from tap to ballet to hip hop for adults and children, ages three and up. It all happens in MET's state-of-the-art home on Caroline Street, which opened in 2013. For beginners, there is a series of six-week intro classes aimed at getting you familiar with the moves. For more experienced dancers, get your tap, ballet, or modern dance fix, starting at just ten dollars per class. Who needs the gym when you can sweat like this?

2808 Caroline St., 713-522-6375
metdance.org

Neighborhood: Midtown

MOUNTAIN BIKE THE
"HO CHI MINH TRAIL"

Behind the ball fields that line the south side of Memorial Drive through Memorial Park, there's a series of trails in a densely wooded area where only the most skilled mountain bikers dare pedal. Though varying topography is difficult to come by in Houston, the terrain here has been carved out along the north bank of Buffalo Bayou, creating natural ravines and sheer, cliff-like drops that make for a dangerous, yet exhilarating, course for the experienced cyclist. The trails aren't long, but know what you're doing and be wary of other cyclists.

6500 Memorial Dr., 713-863-8403
memorialparkconservancy.org

Neighborhood: Uptown

FAST FACT
There are more than three hundred miles of interconnected bike paths and trails spread out across the city of Houston, with many of these running along the city's network of bayous.

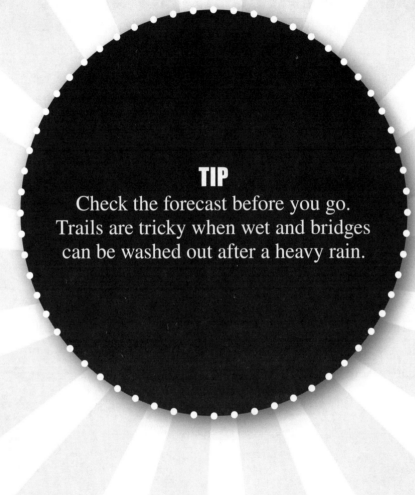

TIP
Check the forecast before you go.
Trails are tricky when wet and bridges
can be washed out after a heavy rain.

KAYAK AN URBAN OASIS
AT BUFFALO BAYOU

Extending northwest from Galveston Bay, Buffalo Bayou wends through the urban landscape of Houston. At one time, the serpentine river was the backbone of the city; the body of water on which Houston was founded also served as its primary means of moving goods through an early port. Today, stretches of the bayou nearest Downtown serve as an urban oasis, offering hundreds of acres of park space and trails. One of the most intriguing ways to experience the bayou is by kayak. Put in downtown at the Sunset Coffee Building at Allen's Landing and work your way toward destinations west. On your journey, you'll discover many different species of birds, one of the state's largest bat colonies (under Waugh Bridge), and other wildlife. If you don't own a kayak, rent one through the Buffalo Bayou Partnership at the Sunset Coffee Building.

buffalobayou.org

Neighborhood: Downtown/Montrose

YELL "FORE!"
AT TOPGOLF

Who says you have to be an expert on the fairway to have fun with a golf club and a ball? The folks at Topgolf certainly don't think so. It all started like this: two brothers on a driving range in London wanted to know exactly how far their drives were traveling. So they created balls containing microchips to track both accuracy and distance. Players compete by aiming their drives at targets in a 240-yard outfield. What makes Topgolf a blast is anyone can do it, from kids to pros. And the abundant food and beverage options delivered to your personal hitting bay—well, that's just icing.

1030 Memorial Brook Blvd., 281-406-3176
topgolf.com/us

Neighborhood: Energy Corridor

SHOW OFF YOUR SKILLS
ON THE ICE AT DISCOVERY GREEN

Ice skating outdoors in Houston? Sure, the weather may be a balmy sixty degrees in December, but that's no reason not to practice your triple axel. Just before the Thanksgiving holiday each year, the folks at Downtown's Discovery Green drain part of the small lake in the park and construct an ice rink that's frozen from underneath the surface. Visitors take to the ice nightly through February, enjoying the pleasure of skating surrounded by the skyscrapers of the business district. Special events, including movie nights on ice, are held throughout the season.

1500 McKinney St., 713-400-7336
discoverygreen.com

Neighborhood: Downtown

READY, AIM, FIRE!
AT ATHENA GUN CLUB

Whether you've never shot a gun before or you're an expert marksman, you're likely to agree that few places offer the kind of indoor shooting experience found at Athena Gun Club. Shooting classes, CHL classes, and even virtual training simulators round out the experience at this upscale West Houston shooting range. The twenty-six-lane, state-of-the-art range is open to members and the public, with hourly rates, as well as accommodations for groups. There's also a full retail store and firearm rental facility for use on the range. But perhaps the most interesting experience at Athena is the "use of force" simulator. Often used by law enforcement personnel, the simulator contains more than 150 dynamic scenarios that give you a way to safely test your shooting skills and reaction times. After all, guns may be a way of life in Texas, but so is using them properly and safely.

10814 Katy Fwy., 713-461-5900
athenagunclub.com

Neighborhood: West Houston

SET SAIL
ON GALVESTON BAY

There's something special about sailing on the open water: the wind, the waves, the synchronized movements needed to propel the boat in the right direction. If you haven't experienced it before, do yourself a favor and head down to Houston's Bay Area. There you'll be able to charter a sailboat or a sailing yacht for the day. Watch dolphins play on Galveston Bay, swim off the beach of a small island, or just enjoy a sunset view on your slice of tranquil paradise. Charter a boat on your own if you're an experienced sailor, or get one equipped with a crew and sit back and enjoy the ride, drink in hand, of course. These sails are perfect for an adventure with friends and family or for a romantic evening under the moonlight.

sailgalvestonbay.com

Neighborhood: Bay Area

GO BIRDING
AT ANAHUAC

When the weather turns colder in the fall, the Upper Texas Coastal Region comes alive with birds migrating south for the winter. Here you'll find wood storks, roseate spoonbills, brown pelicans, and blue herons, among others. At the Anahuac National Wildlife Refuge, you can explore thirty-four thousand acres of meandering bayous and coastal marshes—ideal grounds for alligators, bobcats, and hundreds of species of migratory birds.

4017 FM 563, Anahuac, TX, 409-267-3337
fws.gov/refuge/anahuac

TAKE TO THE AIR
AT SKYDIVE SPACELAND

To celebrate his ninetieth birthday, Houston resident and former President George H.W. Bush jumped out of a plane, just as he had during World War II. So that raises the question: If a ninety-year-old ex-leader of the free world can do it, why can't you? Head south of the city to Skydive Spaceland and experience what it's like to hurtle to the earth at more than 120 miles an hour. The expert team at Spaceland will get you prepped for a tandem jump (for the novice first-timer) or get you trained and certified to skydive solo through a weeklong series of classes. Everything you need, from equipment to instruction—oh, and that perfectly good airplane you're going to jump from—is provided at this private 134-acre facility.

16111 FM 521, Rosharon, TX, 281- 369-3337
houston.skydivespaceland.com

Neighborhood: Bay Area

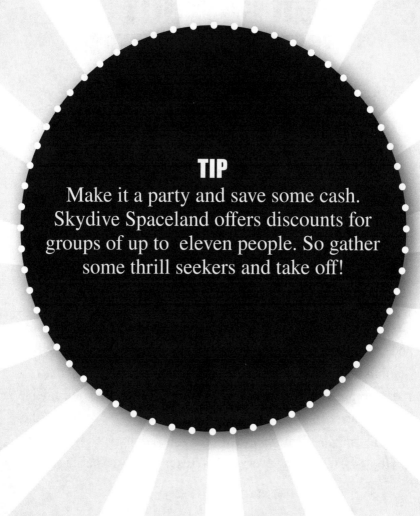

TIP
Make it a party and save some cash. Skydive Spaceland offers discounts for groups of up to eleven people. So gather some thrill seekers and take off!

GO COWBOY
AT THE HOUSTON LIVESTOCK SHOW AND RODEO

If you come to Houston looking for a cowboys-and-roundups version of Texas, you're not likely to find it most of the year. The exception is the first three weeks in March, when the Houston Livestock Show and Rodeo rolls into town. More than 2.5 million people attend the rodeo each year, making it one of the largest in the world. Patrons enjoy a massive midway, food from some of the region's best restaurants, a livestock show that fills an entire convention center, and twenty headline performers in country, pop, and other genres of music. Stars such as Reba McEntire, George Straight, Kenny Chesney, Ariana Grande, John Legend, and many more have played the rodeo's rotating stage at NRG Stadium for up to seventy-five thousand fans. And then there's the rodeo competition itself, which draws the nation's top bull riders, ropers, barrel racers, and other competitors in the sport of the west. During its spring run each year, rodeo dominates the culture of Houston, reminding everyone of Texas's western heritage.

One NRG Park, 832-667-1000
rodeohouston.com

Neighborhood: NRG Park

ROCK THE CRADLE
AT LEE AND JOE JAMAIL SKATEPARK

Skateboarding aficionados know a good skatepark when they see it. And Lee and Joe Jamail is it. The state-of-the-art facility offers thirty-thousand-square-feet of rails, cradles, and bowls for skateboarders looking to show off their mad skills. Areas of the skatepark are set up for boarders of different talent levels, whether you're a novice or a champion at kick flips. When it opened in 2008, the skatepark was hailed as one of the top facilities of its kind in the country, and users say that stature hasn't diminished. Admission to the skatepark, located on the south side of Buffalo Bayou at Sabine Street, is free.

103 Sabine St., 713-222-5500

Neighborhood: Downtown

SHOPPING AND FASHION

DIG FOR TREASURE
AT TEXAS JUNK

Robert Novotney's warehouse-like store in Montrose isn't much to look at. You might even call it a repository of junk. But he's already beat you to it. Texas Junk Company is a packrat's paradise, filled with odds and ends ranging from a massive collection of used boots and vintage frames to tchotchkes and classic vinyl records. If you're in the market for something quirky, this is the place to be. The Texas-centric items often fly off the shelves around rodeo season in March, so keep that in mind if you're hunting for a good pair of broken-in boots. Texas Junk is only open on Fridays and Saturdays, and the pickings are better early.

215 Welch St., 713-524-6257

Neighborhood: Montrose

GET A LOOK
AT HAMILTON SHIRTS

In 1883, brothers Edward and J. Brooke Hamilton opened a shirt company in what was still the relatively small city of Houston. Well over a century later, Hamilton Shirt Company is regarded as one of the finest shirt makers in the United States and the oldest continuously operating business in Houston. The company, now in its fourth generation of Hamilton ownership, crafts made-to-measure and bespoke shirts for locals and men the world over, using a time-honored process. For bespoke shirts, customers are measured to exact specifications in the Houston workshop, and a shirt form is created for the current order and stored for future orders. Hamilton shirts have been worn by statesmen and entertainers, Hollywood heavyweights, and Fortune 500 CEOs.

5700 Richmond Ave., 713-780-8222
hamiltonshirts.com

Neighborhood: Uptown

CRUISE THE CAMPUS
AT KUHL-LINSCOMB

From the outside, it's a deceiving place. One could be excused for thinking Kuhl-Linscomb is just another retail boutique, an unassuming storefront in a small strip of shops in the Upper Kirby District. But the first thing you find upon entering the door is a map, and that's clue number one that this is not your typical shopping experience. The map outlines what you'll find in the multiple bungalow-style buildings that make up the Kuhl-Linscomb campus. This eighty-thousand-square-foot retail wonderland offers gift items and bath products, children's toys and fine china, eclectic furniture and innovative kitchen gadgetry—and that's not the half of it. Husband-wife team Dan and Pam Linscomb have spent years putting together the eclectic mix of merchandise found at their store. And that's led to write-ups in design publications the world over, making Kuhl-Linscomb a destination for interior decorators and the public at large.

2424 W Alabama St., 713-526-6000
kuhl-linscomb.com

Neighborhood: Upper Kirby

BARTER FOR BLOOMS
ON FLOWER ROW

On Fannin Street, between Midtown and the Museum District, just south of the MetroRail crossing, you'll find Flower Row. Here several vendors in huge open-air floral markets hawk beautiful arrangements, plants, and bouquets twenty-four hours a day, seven days a week. The flowers sold here come mostly from Mexico and Central and South America. Once they arrive in the shops, they are fashioned into arrangements for weddings, funerals, and everything in between. Ornate topiaries and large flower-laden bushes line the sides of some of the shops. Flower arranging in these shops is a skill passed from generation to generation. Curiously though, you won't find prices on many of the items here. You have to ask. And that leads to the starting price. It's up to you to offer a different amount and determine whether a deal is struck.

Fannin Street between US 59 and the Museum District

GET FRESH
AT CANINO'S PRODUCE CO.

On Airline Drive just north of the Houston Heights, you'll find Canino Produce Company. This family-run business, founded in 1958, features more than twenty-thousand-square-feet of fresh fruits and vegetables from across Texas, as well as spices, sauces, and other foodstuffs. But the real adventure begins when you exit behind the main building into the open-air Mexican-style market. There you'll find individual vendors offering everything from exotic produce and Mexican cookware to imported spices and specialties like *mango con chile y limon.*

2520 Airline Dr., 713-862-4027
caninoproduce.com

Neighborhood: The Heights

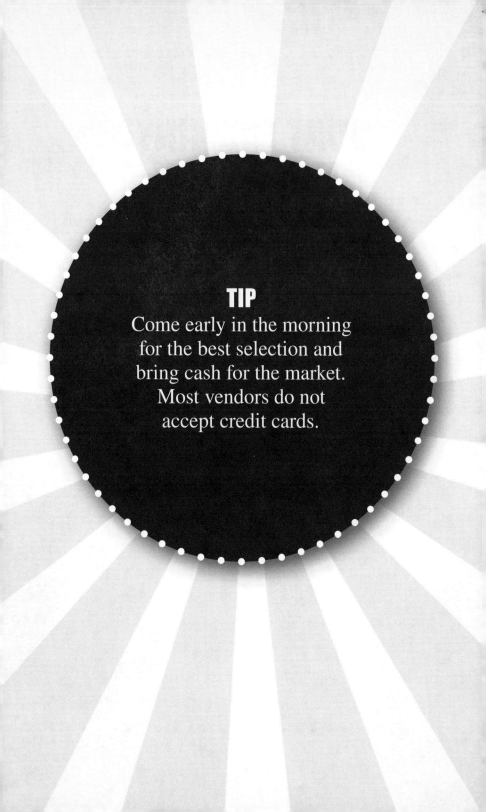

TIP

Come early in the morning
for the best selection and
bring cash for the market.
Most vendors do not
accept credit cards.

HUNT FOR VINYL
AT CACTUS MUSIC

The city's oldest independent music store is still rocking after forty years. That's partly because, in an age of digital downloads and streaming radio, Cactus Music remains old-school. The store hosts weekly "in-store" nights, when local bands come to play for free and sell a few CDs in the process. Long a must-play on Houston's live music circuit, Cactus often rides the line between performance venue and retail shop. It also carries a large array of vintage vinyl records for those lucky enough to have a working turntable. Local music fans cite Cactus as a driving force in Houston's independent scene.

2110 Portsmouth St., 713-526-9272
cactusmusictx.com

Neighborhood: Montrose

BUY A DESIGNER KNOCK-OFF
ON HARWIN DRIVE

Many major cities have neighborhoods, often chaotic and overwhelming, geared toward the deal-finder. Think Chinatown in New York or the Fashion District in L.A. In Houston, that district is Harwin Drive. In this multi-block area, just off the Southwest Freeway, you'll find a labyrinth of wholesale stores, independent vendors, fashion outlets, and more. Whether you're looking for knock-off handbags or perfume, prom dresses or discount designer shoes, jewelry or electronics, there are stores here that specialize in just about anything. Yes, it's overwhelming, and you should definitely do a little homework ahead of time to determine which stores you want to hit up, but for the true bargain hunter, this is a destination that cannot be missed.

Neighborhood: Chinatown

GO ANTIQUING
ON 19TH STREET

19th Street in the historic section of the Houston Heights feels like a slice of small-town America. There are coffee shops and cafés, small grocers, and home-goods stores—a bit of everything, really. And if you're looking for unique furnishings or unusual items, this is the right place. Start at Grace Hart & Company, which houses a group of antique and collectible dealers all under one roof. You'll find century-old china and glass, gadgetry from yesteryear, and more.

313 W 19th St., 713-862-1010

Neighborhood: The Heights

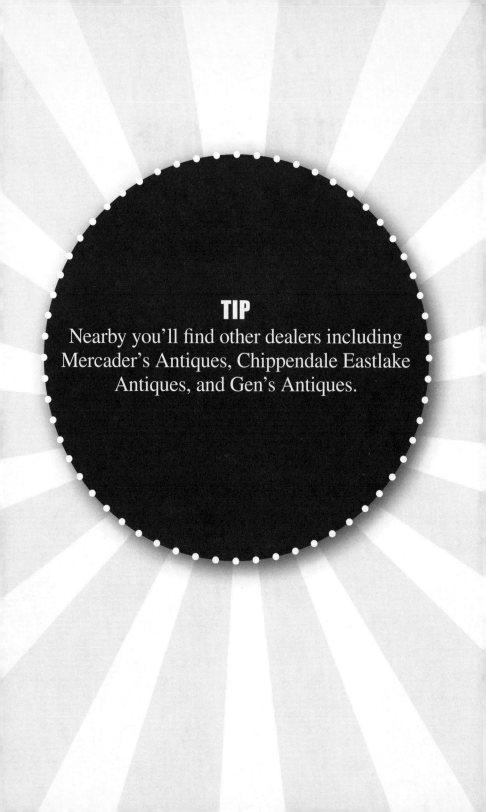

TIP

Nearby you'll find other dealers including Mercader's Antiques, Chippendale Eastlake Antiques, and Gen's Antiques.

GET A PAIR OF CUSTOM BOOTS
AT MAIDA'S

While you won't find a lot of cattle in the big cities of Texas these days, you will find subtle hints of that storied western culture, including beautiful boots on everyone from CEOs to sorority girls. In 1901, a young Italian immigrant named John Maida began making boots in downtown Houston. More than a century later, his family continues the tradition at Maida's, handcrafting custom-made boots with premium leathers from around the world. Each pair is designed with input from the buyer and can incorporate features such as inlaying, overlaying, and lacing. That kind of attention to detail doesn't come cheap: you're likely to spend more than $700 for a solid pair of boots that can take ten to twelve weeks to make. But with proper care, they'll last forever. Maida's clients have included a number of celebrities such as members of the rock band ZZ Top.

By appointment only. 3948 Westheimer, 713-315-7595
maidas.com

SHOP 'TIL YOU DROP
AT THE GALLERIA

It's a mall, right? What's the big deal? Oh, my friend, The Galleria isn't just a mall: it's a full-blown three million-square-foot, four-hundred-store, all-day experience. Opened in 1970 and modeled after the Galleria Vittorio Emanuele II in Milan, The Galleria today is the largest mall in Texas and continues to add to its footprint. Luxury shops such as Prada, Neiman Marcus, Saks Fifth Avenue, Tiffany & Co., and Fendi mix with more mainstream stores like Banana Republic, Express, and The Gap. One of the defining characteristics of The Galleria is its full-size ice skating rink. With two hotels connected to the mall, along with a post office and children's play area, The Galleria is a veritable city unto itself.

5085 Westheimer Rd., 713-966-3500
galleriahouston.com

Neighborhood: Uptown

TAKE A SHORT TRIP TO THE FAR EAST
AT HONG KONG CITY MALL

One of the centerpieces of Houston's vast Chinatown neighborhood is Hong Kong City Mall. With more than twenty restaurants and small cafés and dozens of additional shops and services, the mall is a hub of activity for the city's large Asian community and others looking for authentic food and goods. Hong Kong City Mall is anchored by HK Food Market, an expansive grocery filled with exotic produce and imported fare. This is far from your typical American grocer, so prepare for a real cultural experience. Outside of the market, you'll find Vietnamese bakeries and bubble tea cafés in addition to gift shops, jewelry stores, and foot massage spas, just to name a few things. Capping the west end of the center is Ocean Palace restaurant, where you'll taste some of the best dim sum in the city. Hong Kong City Mall is also the site of a number of Asian cultural events and activities.

11205 Bellaire Blvd.
hkcitymall.com

Neighborhood: Chinatown

TIP

Many of the restaurants and cafés in Chinatown do not accept credit or debit cards, so it's a good idea to go with cash if you want to sample your way through the area.

MUSIC AND ENTERTAINMENT

HEAR LEGENDS PLAY
AT FITZGERALD'S

On any given night of the week, the intersection of White Oak and Studemont in the Heights neighborhood is buzzing with music fans eager to catch the latest act at Fitzgerald's. Over the last four decades, Fitz's has become one of the most iconic music venues in Houston. Performers such as the legendary rock band ZZ Top got their start here, and the spot has hosted such talent as James Brown, Tina Turner, and the Ramones. The building itself has its own storied history, serving as a gathering place for the city's Polish immigrant community for sixty years before Sarah Fitzgerald turned it into her namesake concert venue in 1977. Big shows happen upstairs on the main stage, while more intimate shows take the mic on the first level. For today's up-and-coming Houston musicians, playing Fitz's is a rite of passage and a sign that they're on their way.

2706 White Oak Dr., 713-862-3838
fitzlivemusic.com

Neighborhood: The Heights

GO BATTY
AT WAUGH BRIDGE

Most nights of the year, visitors to a Buffalo Bayou overlook can glimpse a unique spectacle as the second largest urban colony of Mexican free-tailed bats in Texas emerges to feed. Bats get a bad rap, but these mammals of the sky are virtually harmless to humans and, in fact, help keep the population of mosquitoes and other insects in check. A single colony, like the roughly 250,000 under Waugh Bridge, can consume tons of insects in a week. The overlook at Allen Parkway and Waugh provides the perfect perch to watch the bats form a fast-moving cloud. Buffalo Bayou Partnership also offers regular pontoon boat rides to watch the takeoff. The colony emerges at sunset but may delay flight if the weather is bad or if the temperature is below fifty degrees. Get there a bit earlier to ensure you don't miss the show.

Intersection of Montrose Blvd. and Allen Pkwy.
houstontx.gov/parks/batpage.html

Neighborhood: Montrose

DO THE TWO-STEP
AT WILD WEST

Few things say Texas quite like a classic honky-tonk. There are more than a few in the Houston area, but Wild West is an institution that's been around more than thirty years. You shouldn't expect nothin' too fancy from a place where the motto is "two steppin' and longneckin." But at Wild West you'll find a large solid oak dance floor, the latest and the classics of country tunes, and, of course, a well-stocked bar with friendly bartenders. Free dance lessons are available every Sunday afternoon for those wanting to learn all the right moves. And stick around for the family-style fajita dinner. The bar is located on the Richmond Strip, just west of the Galleria area.

6101 Richmond Ave., 713-266-3455
wildwesthouston.com

Neighborhood: Uptown

OTHER POPULAR HONKY-TONKS

Armadillo Palace
5015 Kirby Dr., 713-526-9700
goodecompany.com/palace.asp

Alice's Tall Texan
4904 N Main, 713-862-0141

Firehouse Saloon
5930 Southwest Fwy., 713-977-1962
firehousesaloon.com

Mo's Place
21940 Kingsland Blvd., Katy, TX
281-392-3499
mosplacekaty.com

LIVE LIKE A KING
AT THE TEXAS RENAISSANCE FESTIVAL

Hear ye, hear ye! Take a journey back to the Middle Ages, when knights fought for the affection of a fair maiden and kings' conquests included—turkey legs? The Texas Renaissance Festival is spread out across fifty-five acres near Magnolia, about an hour northwest of downtown Houston. This is one of the oldest and most well-established Renaissance festivals in the country, drawing well over half a million people each fall over the course of its eight-week run. The festival includes a large-scale jousting arena, falconry demonstrations, hundreds of merchants, gardens, restaurants, taverns, multiple-themed areas, and even elephant rides. Performers entertain the crowds with everything from juggling to acrobatics. Meanwhile, period-specific costumes and authentic scenery transport revelers to a time long ago. There are even medieval wedding packages—in case you want to tie the knot with a lord or lady.

21778 FM Rd. 1774, Todd Mission, TX, 281-356-2178
texrenfest.com

RENT A B-CYCLE
AND EXPLORE

With numerous trails and dedicated cycling lanes, one of the best ways to experience Houston is by bike. In 2012, the city launched a new bike sharing program dubbed B-Cycle. Today there are well over thirty stations from Downtown to Buffalo Bayou and the Heights to Montrose, allowing users to check out bikes by the hour, for a full day, or even with a yearly membership. When you're done with the bike, simply check it back in at one of the stations. Want to take a nice long ride? Hit the trail from Downtown along Buffalo Bayou to Montrose. Next go north to Hermann Park and the Museum District before heading back toward Downtown through Midtown.

Houston.bcycle.com

SHOW YOUR PATRIOTISM
AT FREEDOM OVER TEXAS

One of the largest single-day events in Houston, Freedom Over Texas is an annual patriotic celebration like no other. It all happens in Eleanor Tinsley Park, set against the backdrop of the downtown skyline, where nearly fifty thousand people gather to hear headliners like Martina McBride and Sheryl Crow. A beer garden, kids' zone, dozens of food options, and five stages of entertainment make this a hot ticket. There's even an area dedicated to Houston's pro sports teams, where the kids can pick up some soccer skills with a Dynamo player and throw with a pitcher from the Astros. When the sun goes down, the entertainment is capped off with fireworks over Buffalo Bayou, one of the largest displays in the country.

Houstontx.gov/july4

TWO-WHEEL IT
ON A SEGWAY TOUR

The world looks a little different standing on two wheels. If you've never taken a Segway tour, don't be intimidated. The vehicles are easy to operate and quite fun, once you get the hang of it. Take a ride with Segway Tours of Houston along Buffalo Bayou or through Downtown to some of the city's more interesting historic sites. You'll be led on these roughly two-hour tours by one of the company's knowledgeable guides, who are eager to share and point out things easily missed by the casual observer.

713-522-1200
Segwaytoursofhouston.com

Neighborhood: Downtown

KNOCK TO JOIN THE PARTY
AT LAST CONCERT CAFÉ

Amid the warehouses and art studios that line the streets between north Downtown and I-10, there stands a single-story Spanish-style building with a clay tile roof and bright red door. You have to knock for entry here, which is part of the experience of this unusual little Mexican restaurant. The meals are simple: chicken enchiladas, beef fajitas, flautas topped with guacamole. Last Concert Café does a brisk lunch business among the lawyers, judges, and others with offices nearby. But after the sun goes down, that's when this place gets really interesting. With margaritas flowing, the party moves to the large patio and yard out back, dominated by a stage. This is where many local musicians have cut their teeth and many a fan has danced (and even hula hooped) to the beat. This building, which was once a speakeasy—and some say a bordello—now draws a regular crowd of music lovers looking for the next emerging band.

1403 Nance St., 713-226-8563
lastconcert.com

Neighborhood: Downtown

PLAY TOURIST
ON A DOUBLE-DECKER BUS

You could be forgiven for thinking you're in London after seeing Houston City Tours' double-decker buses roaming the streets of H-Town. These hop-on, hop-off buses provide riders a perfect perch to see the city sites, from locations of historical and cultural significance Downtown to the attractions of the Museum District. Buses pick up and drop off at each of six stops every ninety minutes, three times a day, starting at 10 a.m.

832-388-8434
houstoncitytours.us

DISCOVER A HIDDEN CURIOSITY
AT THE BAYOU BUBBLE

It's often referred to as the Big Bubble, and sometimes the Bayou Burp. But it's not the sort of thing you'll find on maps of attractions around town. On the southeastern edge of the Preston Street Bridge over Buffalo Bayou, there's a small red button, almost hidden in the brick column that caps the bridge. No sign identifies this unusual feature, and certainly more than one person has been a little perplexed by its presence. But if you press the button, a gas pocket is released from beneath the waters of the bayou below, resulting in an eruption of large bubbles lasting several seconds. Artist Dean Ruck, who created the Big Bubble, intentionally wanted it to be discreet—a feature people happened upon without necessarily knowing what it was. He says the button plays upon the curiosity of us all: Dare we push it and find out what happens?

515 Preston St.

Neighborhood: Downtown

TIP
From the end of the bridge,
you can't actually see the bubbles
produced by pressing the button,
so it's best to go with someone
and take turns pressing and
checking out the results.

PLAY WITH SOUND
AT THE DISCOVERY GREEN LISTENING VESSELS

On the southern edge of the downtown park, Discovery Green, you'll find a peculiar pair of circular stone sculptures. There's no sign here explaining what to do, and the casual observer might simply dismiss the structures as strange art, but locals know the pieces hold a special secret. These are the Listening Vessels created by artist Doug Hollis. Carved from Alabama limestone, the large concave discs situated some seventy feet apart actually focus sound waves, allowing a person to speak softly inside one vessel and be heard distinctly by someone sitting in the other. The Listening Vessels are just one interactive component of the twelve-acre Discovery Green Park, which opened to the public in 2008 and anchors the city's Convention District. Here visitors find playgrounds, a rotation of art exhibits, a dog park, and a small lake for kayaking and model boats. Live music takes to the amphitheater stage on weekends, and outdoor ice skating is a holiday favorite.

1500 McKinney St., 713-400-7336
discoverygreen.com

Neighborhood: Downtown

CATCH AN INDIE FLICK
AT RIVER OAKS THEATRE

Opened in 1939, the River Oaks Theatre is a classic example of art deco design. The theater is an anchor of the River Oaks Shopping Center, one of the first vehicle-centric shopping centers built in the United States, neighboring the palatial homes of posh River Oaks. With its hand-lettered neon marquee, sidewalk ticket window, and three screens—one large downstairs and two smaller upstairs—the theater harkens back to a time before the megaplex. Here patrons see the latest art house and foreign-language films as well as the occasional blockbuster. One thing not to be missed: the monthly, second-Saturday screening of the Rocky Horror Picture Show at midnight. Don't be afraid to dress up—you definitely won't be alone.

2009 West Gray St., 713-866-8881
landmarktheatres.com/houston/river-oaks-theatre

Neighborhood: River Oaks

TAKE A PREHISTORIC SAFARI
AT THE HOUSTON MUSEUM OF NATURAL SCIENCE

Most paleontology exhibits in museums feature dinosaur skeletons lined up one after the other. But when the Houston Museum of Natural Science opened its Hall of Paleontology in 2012, they set out to do something new: to recreate actual encounters between dinosaurs as they might have happened millions of years ago. The result is a real adventure, where visitors see actual fossil mounts in action—eating, chasing, fighting, and flying— next to large-scale panoramic paintings of these same encounters. Around every corner in this football field-sized hall, you discover a new scene in the life-and-death battle that characterized the prehistoric era. Visitors trace the evolutionary timeline from the earliest forms of life to the dinosaurs, all the way to the earliest man. The paleo hall is just one of many experiences at the Houston Museum of Natural Science, which also includes a full-scale planetarium, a massive gem and jewelry vault, a stunning indoor rainforest inhabited by thousands of butterflies, an exhibit dedicated to ancient Egypt, and much more.

5555 Hermann Park Dr., 713-639-4629
hmns.org

Neighborhood: Museum District

SLEEP LIKE A LEGEND
IN THE MAGNIFICENT SEVEN SUITES AT HOTEL ZAZA

Rock stars take notice: Houston has a hotel room with your name on it. Literally. Whether it's the Rock Star Suite, with its mirrored walls and elaborate fireplace, or the twenty-two-hundred-square-foot Black Label Suite, with its two-person tub on the balcony and large gray crystal chandelier, the Magnificent Seven Suites offer paramount pampering. Each of the well-appointed suites has a unique, yet consistently high-end, aesthetic. With a perch overlooking the Museum District and Hermann Park, Hotel ZaZa is perfectly positioned for those looking to experience some of the best attractions in town. And if it's a theme you want, the hotel has that too. Spend a night in the "Houston, We Have a Problem" suite, with its 1960s space-mod look, or the red-soaked "Geisha House," with its pagoda poster bed and teak-laden shower.

5701 Main St., 713-526-1991
hotelzaza.com

Neighborhood: Museum district

ROCK ON
AT FREE PRESS SUMMER FEST

Free Press Summer Fest is Houston's largest live music festival. Launched in 2009 with an attendance of about 30,000 over two days, the festival today draws more than 100,000 fans to Eleanor Tinsley Park on the banks of Buffalo Bayou. Bands, many of them Texas-based, perform on multiple stages set up around the park. Fireworks and local food are other consistent elements of the event, which typically takes place the first weekend in June. National performers including Jack White, Vampire Weekend, Dwight Yoakum, Snoop Dogg, and Alabama Shakes have previously performed at Free Press Summer Fest. The local independent newspaper *Free Press Houston* produces the festival in conjunction with promoter Pegstar.

fpsf.com

TRACK GREAT APES
AT GORILLAS OF THE AFRICAN FOREST

Emerging from a thick forest of trees, a male lowland gorilla saunters toward you, a mass of muscle with a face full of expression, and only a clear glass panel separates the two of you. That's the experience at Gorillas of the African Forest, an immersive exhibit that opened at the Houston Zoo in spring 2015. One of the largest and most innovative habitats for captive gorillas in the world, this $35 million exhibit offers multiple vantage points, including a treetop trail, to view gorillas as they exist in the wild. It's the latest installation in the zoo's massive African Forest experience, which aims to take visitors on a realistic safari as they see chimpanzees, rhinos, and other animals in habitats closely resembling their wild environments.

6200 Hermann Park Dr., 713-533-6500
houstonzoo.org

Neighborhood: Museum District

TAKE A PHOTOGRAPHY CLASS
AT HOUSTON CENTER FOR PHOTOGRAPHY

Of course you have a camera, but do you really know how to use it? The Learning Center at Houston Center for Photography offers a myriad of courses and workshops each season for film and digital photographers of all skill levels. The classes are presented on-site at HCP out in the field or at the facilities of HCP partner organizations. Some of the workshops are single-day sessions, but others take place over the course of several weeks, depending on the skills being taught. A few of the dozens of classes offered include photographing at night, lighting in photography, photojournalism, and building your photography portfolio. So whether you're just trying to advance your everyday photo skills or attempting to build a photography business, the Learning Center at HCP has a class to help you get there.

1441 W Alabama St., 713-529-4755
hcponline.org

Neighborhood: Museum District

TOUR THE TUNNELS
WITH "THE TUNNEL LADY"

It might not be the most flattering moniker to some, but Sandra Lord wears the title "Tunnel Lady" like a badge of honor. For decades, the professional tour guide has led locals and out-of-towners alike on a tour of the seven-and-a-half miles of tunnels underneath downtown Houston. Constructed in phases over the years, starting in the 1960s, the tunnels enable downtown workers to get around without ever setting foot outside (a blessing during the height of summer). Down below is a veritable city unto itself, with dozens of restaurants, shops, and services from banks to beauty shops. Lord's tour showcases the history of the tunnels and takes you to some of the best eateries along the way.

discoverhoustontours.com

Neighborhood: Downtown

MAKE OUT UPSTAIRS
AT MARFRELESS

It takes a little extra effort to find the nondescript blue door in the rear of the River Oaks Shopping Center. But the speakeasy vibe is part of the charm of Marfreless. Once you're in, you've got a beautiful long, solid-wood bar with plenty of libations to choose from. But the real attraction of Marfreless is upstairs. That's where you'll find cozy little nooks where couples make out—and it's been that way since the establishment's founding in 1972. Certainly, more than a few mistresses have been spirited away to this convenient little spot for a date. But anyone who sees you amorously involved here is probably up to something themselves.

2006 Peden St., 832-315-1495
Marfrelesshouston.com

Neighborhood: River Oaks

RIDE THE BEAST
AT KEMAH

In the small bayside community of Kemah is the Kemah Boardwalk, an amusement park offering quite a few thrills. But perhaps the biggest is known as the Boardwalk Beast. The twenty-five-minute thrill ride on Galveston Bay reaches speeds of up to forty miles per hour. If you think there's a chance you won't get wet, think again. The captain's goal is to ensure everyone gets a good soaking. The music, the wind, and the speed all combine to make this a ride to remember. After all, they don't call it the beast for nothing.

215 Kipp Ave., Kemah, TX, 281-535-8100
kemahboardwalk.com

Neighborhood: Bay Area Houston

STARGAZE
AT GEORGE OBSERVATORY

"For my part, I know nothing with any certainty, but the sight of stars makes me dream." Vincent van Gogh certainly had the right idea. Mankind has been captivated and inspired by the night sky for millennia, and today we can get closer to the stars than ever before, thanks to technology. About an hour's drive south of the city, inside Brazos Bend State Park, you'll find the trio of domes that house the George Observatory. Open to visitors each Saturday afternoon and evening year-round, this satellite facility of the Houston Museum of Natural Science allows guests to view celestial bodies through a series of research telescopes. Volunteer astronomers are on site during each viewing to answer questions and guide users in finding key elements in the sky, from the Milky Way to the cloud belts of Jupiter. Visitors who arrive early can even check out the sun using the facility's special solar scope. The observatory also holds astronomy classes and special events each season.

21901 FM 762 Rd., Needville, TX
hmns.org

Neighborhood: Fort Bend County

GET HIGHER
AT CHASE TOWER

Want a birds-eye view of the city from its tallest skyscraper? At seventy-five gleaming stories, the Chase Tower office building rises high over the center of downtown Houston. And during regular business hours, Monday through Friday, visitors to the building can take the express elevators from the lobby up to the observation deck on the tower's sixtieth floor. From this vantage point, visitors can see Downtown in panorama as well as The Galleria, the Texas Medical Center and NRG Park. On a clear day, you may even be able to sight the Houston Ship Channel and the San Jacinto Monument in the far distance. Luckily, the dramatic view is free. Lunch afterwards at a nearby restaurant? That will cost you.

600 Travis St.
chasetower.com

TAKE A FREE BOAT RIDE
ON THE SHIP CHANNEL

Who doesn't like a free tour? Six days a week, the Port of Houston Authority offers ninety-minute round-trip cruises along the Houston Ship Channel, allowing passengers to see one of the world's busiest ports at work. The tour boat *M/V Sam Houston* can take up to ninety passengers at a time on the tour from Sam Houston Pavilion to the Turning Basin Terminal and back. The tours have been offered for more than fifty years, providing a first-hand view of ships carrying cargo from all over the world as well as oceangoing tankers, and other vessels. Tour participants also get to see how cargo is loaded and unloaded at terminals along the channel.

7300 Clinton Dr., 713-670-2416
portofhouston.com

Neighborhood: East End

TIP

Tours are available every day of the week except for Mondays, and although the tour is free, advanced reservations are required.

TAKE A SELFIE
AT THE WATER WALL

Just steps from The Galleria mall in the Uptown district, the Gerald D. Hines Water Wall is simply a fun place to hang out. The sixty-four-foot semicircular fountain cycles eleven thousand gallons of water per minute down its inner and outer walls. The Water Wall is an architectural gem surrounded by the Water Wall Park, a nearly three-acre site dotted by dozens of live oak trees, creating a perfect place to picnic, take photos—and even pop the question (more than a few grooms-to-be have done it). Constructed in 1983 as a complement to the nearby office building now dubbed Williams Tower, the Water Wall's height of sixty-four feet pays homage to the tower's sixty-four stories.

2800 Post Oak Blvd.

Neighborhood: Uptown

WATCH A MOVIE UNDER THE STARS
AT MARKET SQUARE PARK

On the north side of Downtown sits Market Square Park. Once a thriving marketplace in Houston's early days and the site of the original City Hall, Market Square became a park decades ago. In 2010, it underwent a complete renovation that brought an event lawn, gardens, public art, a dog park, and even a small restaurant kiosk. The overhaul of the park proved a catalyst for revitalization of this historic part of Downtown. Now the Downtown District programs concerts, bingo, film screenings, and other events seasonally on the park's lawn. Movies on the big inflatable screen range from classics like *Casablanca* to modern cult-films like *Office Space*. So bring a blanket, order up some wine, and enjoy a night of entertainment in the open air.

301 Milam St., 713-223-2003
marketsquarepark.com

Neighborhood: Downtown

HEAR HOW IT ALL DEVELOPED
WITH AUDIO WALKING TOURS

Downtown Houston is full of unique places and spots of historical significance, but it's not always easy to spot them without a little guidance. Enter Downtown Mobile Info, a self-guided audio tour that users can take using their smartphones. It's pretty simple: you log onto the site and call the number provided. You can then use the map on the mobile site to explore nineteen different sites around the western half of Downtown, from City Hall to the group of seventy-foot sculptures along Buffalo Bayou dubbed the Seven Wonders. The tour is perfect for those who like to explore at their own pace. Be sure to check out the fifth stop on the tour, "Sounds of the Past." As you stand on this spot overlooking Buffalo Bayou, you'll hear the faint sound of an old steamboat whistle. The whistle recording is activated by a motion sensor on the overlook, allowing passersby to experience an earlier time in the city, when goods were shipped up the winding bayou.

houstondmi.org

ACTIVITIES
BY SEASON

WINTER

Catch a Play at Alley Theatre, 26

Test Your Skills at a Chili Cook-Off, 8

Go Cowboy at the Houston Livestock Show and Rodeo, 88

Do the Song and Dance at Theatre Under the Stars, 41

SPRING

Go Birding at Anahuac, 85

Hear How It All Developed with Audio Walking Tours, 137

Get Fresh at Canino's Produce Co., 96

Trace the Evolution of Texas Ranch Life at George Ranch
Historical Park, 61

Savor the Flavor at the Haute Wheels Food Truck Festival, 11

SUMMER

AUTUMN

INDEX